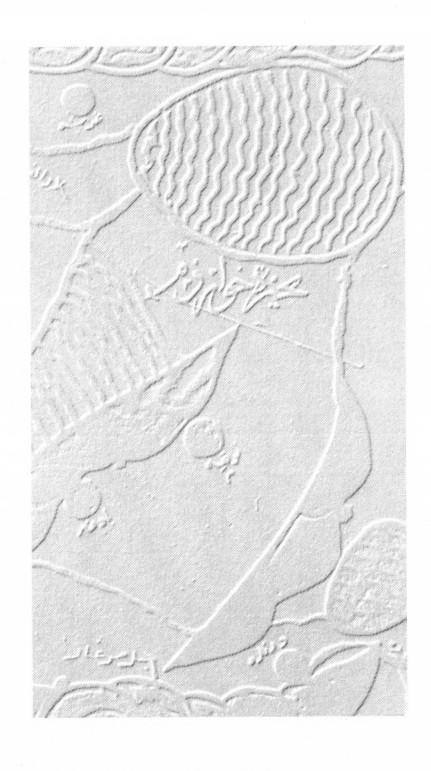

Cartographies of Silence

BY THE AUTHOR

Endings / Round Lake Press, 1990

Cartographies of Silence

Erik Vatne

BARRYTOWN
STATION HILL

Published by Barrytown/Station Hill Press, Inc., 120 Station Hill Road,
Barrytown, NY 12507, as a project of the Institute for Publishing Arts, Inc.,
in Barrytown, New York, a not-for-profit, tax-exempt organization [501(c)(3)],
supported in part by grants from the New York State Council on the Arts.

Online catalogue and purchasing: www.stationhill.org
e-mail: publishers@stationhill.org

Typeset by www.tattfoostudio.com
Front cover and page 155: Axial Drawing (10/1/08) by George Quasha
Back cover: photograph by Dylan Thompson
Project Manager: Jennifer L. Poole

Library of Congress Cataloging-in-Publication Data

Vatne, Erik.
   Cartographies of silence / Erik Vatne.
      p. cm.
   Poems.
   ISBN 978-1-58177-113-8 (alk. paper)
   I. Title.

PS3622.A88C37 2009
811'.6--dc22

                              2008049498

Manufactured in the United States of America.

For my mother

"*A man will be imprisoned in a room with a door that's unlocked and opens inwards, as long as it does not occur to him to pull rather than push.*"

—Ludwig Wittgenstein

Cartographies of Silence

writing down

talking down to her

talk down

down below

where it counts

one thing after another

let her speak
let her write down

she will talk down

you will hear

either ether
or witness
or testify

to the heart's
absence

you will listen
behind a door

glass in your hand

music returns

with its distant smoke
and night's endless tautology

open up
to where
you will go

if you take me
with you this time

wait for me

with eyes closed

a hand moves

somewhere
on a page

now isn't the time

try later

it'll be safe

still writing
from the outside yourself

a man risen

vulture

when the book
is opened
something
happens

for better
or worse
something
happens

and there
is no
going
back

my hands hurt

from the weather
and the anger

I am a man in a room

waiting

for the rain

that open hand

fingers
keep curling up
into a fist

have to heat them

---

my hands reach out to you

silent forgeries

I want something

I can almost feel it

almost know it
inside myself

what is it?

this thing lurking behind the words?

he wants to write
as he sleeps

a sentinel
of snow

ambushed by words

doesn't like how they feel

needs to move on
and accept the next word

on faith

no esoteric
candy story

returning to words
after a long exile

elusive fragments
of decoded texts

just let go of them

hall of words

opens out into a long room

coax them out

whisper occasions

torch song

corpus albicans

gizmo

---

and for this

well

you know

synapse

metabolism

a word I can use later

there is enough noise in your head

ash

words

in the dark
like secret lovers

seducing you

until the conversion
is made complete

my defenses are down

a broken player piano
in storage somewhere

let the words in

now while you still can

before it's too late

ragweed

crickets

hum of air conditioner

even a little light
somewhere inside

behind the closed eyes

in a dark room

back there behind the other spaces

the words emerge

move me closer to the window

I can't see

you started believing their language

and then the sickness came
or at least that's what they called it

but you know better

she wasn't worth it

the words
and the energy

so much invested

so much language

so much life lost

I ask for little else

a witness

I want to arrange this
if you can

wordscrowdedtogether

filling the spaces
with words

you have to
say something

you have to
at least try

silences adjust
according to the semantic interloper

primordial regret

to anyone would care to look

who made a fetish out of silence

your emptiness was your beauty
and your mystery

I lusted after those spaces between us

arriving at myself

I speak

I transgress against the silence
of Cézanne's apples

thorax driven snow

by this he means

a window

a word
onto a world

a wedding
of sleep

will you listen
to the sound
of that willow tree
swaying
back and forth
in its sleep

summer night
in a suburban paradise

you know it's true

I can bring you home
I can just wait

wade

a while here

in the place pre-
determined by you

maybe I'll even

you had amnesia for a while

you had aphasia too

you turned your head away

an orb of sound seduces you towards sleep

don't sing too loud

they're sleeping

if only
if only

it was like this

always

here
now

at this moment

hour of the wolf

the night ordains me
in a baptism of snow

hysteria

inertia of objects
induced
by sleepless space

signals

who is watching?

convulsive deprivation

doesn't answer

an organism instead
has an announcement to make

you must sleep now

he makes weird

books

end

as sleep
waits

patiently

for him
to let go

into the darker

into the without light

the rain stick

a talisman

I can't sleep

wood thrush

it's futile
to try and make yourself
feel something

bring me back to my body

everything already inside me

open me up

so I can find those doors
in the spaces inside my body
that no one knows about

I know they are there

my body
a story
waiting
to be told

the time you need in your body
to do your work here

my body
an exploding *stupa*

my breath
a sutra of silence

or in the spaces between

opening your whole attention

while listening

touching

breath

inner being

focus

feel the sound

blessed audibly

saturated with passive form

my body will break open

next time

you will feel the body of space
inside this body

advance into the light

many things in a bed

or even in a body

I can't talk about

I can only dream about

a body in a bed in a room

is how it begins

and a body in a bed in a room

is how it ends

with God
I attained complete tissue saturation

every cell fiber muscle organ etc.

made manifest in the illuminata

12, 045 skies

1, 716 weeks

75 trillion cells

when you turn the page
the book rejects your advances

the book recedes

the book plucks out your eyes

the book can't bear to be read
by them anyway

a topical ointment

ailment

a salve even

like a balm

word medicine

for the wounds

I'm sorry I couldn't make their acquaintance

the words I mean

I was busy with things that are not words

a lip of snow

edema

I am under the influence
always of some esoteric censor

to dance

to move between

shaking the poison
out of my body

shaking my body out of my body too

deep fascia

austerities

the white arcades

canopies

her esoteric smile

tinnitus

try saying yes

venom magic

channels
isn't necessary

it's about movement

a series of closed eyes/

texts

you are a blind man
feeling your way towards something

it has always been this way

it will always be

from this bed

I can see the pines
outside the window

hear the clock ticking
on the night table

I don't know where these things are
in relation to me

I sense something above me

above the bed even
above the music

that something is

did you hear that?

did you hear the dead air?

that's where you live

you should remove your clothes
and walk away

it's not in here

walking again towards that place

each step

your first and last step

on the earth

never to be repeated

better even than walking

on water

too much stimulation

how to discern

sift

censor

not enough space
let pass through

shape shifting
in the dark

the mind crosses the threshold

wanders
into unknown territory

impulses

it contains whatever

it is certain

resemblances

to outside forces

that may be hostile
to your interrogation

turn off that light

it's not dark enough yet

under that door
the blue light from the television

somewhere

transmission

they are knocking

let them in
I have nothing to hide

they can't take anything away from me

I have no enemies outside myself
I have no enemies inside myself

go ahead

let them in

voice of dark stone

in her pocket

at the bottom of the song

the muddy river flows

in the opposite direction

of a door is knocked on

by a boy who enters

a deep cello ignites
the catafalque

a grid
a glyph
a graph

an auction

and then life busts in

fucks the whole thing up

please don't go

I'm not finished with you yet

they are tired
they are tired of saying goodbye to him

in order

out of order

inside

outside

my side

your side

his side

out there

is not

in here

in here

is not

out there

you are

certain

of nothing

tissue saturation takes place
at a certain time a blind man
gropes in the dark stasis of
essential narcoerotic understanding

the breath of the interlocutor
interrogating me

collision

collusion

corrosion

contusion

confusion

concealment

God deepens my pain

a butterfly at the Bronx Zoo

contains the unbearable silence
of Persephone's lust

sacraments

all of a sudden
I could feel his pain

the pain of being

no place

a place for him?

there is a place

a place to be

the next woman I love
will let me be a child in her arms

there are no words
and without them

there is nothing

---

to be engaged with

testify

testimonial

admonition

to make tears distinguish
between clusters
of lapis lazuli light

days
I had to do nothing

but listen

it has to reveal itself

manifest itself
accordingly

reborn

both sexes
inside me

in my dream

a woman
running after me

pissing while she runs

chasing me
over the scarp

what have I done to her?
what have I done to anybody?

God resin

clusters

the rim
of the cracked egg cup

(I do things
with my mind
you wouldn't believe)

I want God to let go of me
so I can become Him

but I'm not ready yet

He isn't ready yet either

restless leg syndrome

claustrophobia

hypochondria

I'm just doing the whole human thing

approaching

yawning

arriving

actualizing

you can cross
things out

do over

design a world

a long road

nexus

parousia

They are talking over our heads

politicized

Paideuma

the rain falls

a day to lie in the warmth
of your own arms

dreaming of loves

listening to Bach

I need a day

to reflect
on falling rain

nothing lasts that doesn't
live long enough

by slow degrees
of light

nothing there for you anyway

don't make me do it

moving towards the opaque
and obsolete

insignia
of your death

it's all right

the dialogue with yourself

that distinguishes this

from that inconsolable action

you are oblivious to

the rain is falling

is there any other way to say that?

stroke your flesh with your right hand

the left one

the one on your hairy leg now

voices

no light

rain

always rain

I didn't mean it

Said

Wrote

Thought

Willed

Dreamed

Prayed

too much heat
and noise

I need a narcotic

a sacrifice

a sacrifice
is always necessary

opening the sacrum

you can adjust

you can change

you can yawn

you can stretch

touch yourself

are you still there?

she places the placenta in the bird feeder

for those birds she knows by sight and sound

but not by name

she feeds the birds her placenta

and they eat it

no questions asked

in between tomorrow

a telephone

a telephone rings

people talk on the other end

where does that end end?

and what happens

when we stop talking?

They are singing over our heads

summer

and he still has his
Christmas lights up

he likes the lights

the blue
the yellow
the green
the red

to see them
in the sky of his room

pre-digested protein

globules

a melanoma
on Rimbaud's knee

whatever the day calls for

flecks of mica
washed away in a summer rain

ginger root

radiology

the silent apples
actualizing

the other machine

archives

voices

follicles

tumescent light

oils

bark/leaves/petals/
resins/rinds/roots/
seeds/stalks/stems

cypress trees

what can come out of that
catastrophe of reason and benediction

but a not honoring the rhythm?

where are my things
and how do I get them back?

and how much are they worth?

and do I need them?

and why do I have them in the first place?

absolved by love

your whole life
is organized
around your pain

séances of undisclosed origin
erupt in her face

and then recede

almost elegantly

they tricked me

a placebo
like god

any of it is real

restless manifestos
of lust

silenced

by the musical
interlocutor

the serpent at the base of your spine

sleeping

the cracked spine of a book

open it

a synapse
presupposes
the extinction
of our lustful alchemy

in the dark
a Barbie doll imposter

Buddha waves us on

intermission

intermezzo

soprano

sonata

snot of assignation

incredulous equals himself

sex staved off for now

words might get in the way

a mirror too might get you confused

make you think you're seeing yourself

my lust was inexorable sadness

and knowing I was lost
your eyes smile at me

brown walnut banister

molasses

Brooklyn

smell of that house

processionals
of sunken ash

sticky secretions
of rain

with a bell like tone

the rain
has tongues
of sleep
to listen to

it snows in the room

it does things like that

it musicks

tissue

  saturation

  musick

on the wing

spine

  ekstasis

it was over

he knew it

he waited for further instruction

a word
a signal

but nothing happened

the book closes

the book collapses
in on itself

until there is nothing

but ash

and then it ends

or simply

too much invested

turn the page

it is your life
you are reading

when you turn the page
you will let go of the past

and in that moment

everything
abandoned me

Acknowledgments

This book was composed in 1995-1996 in New Jersey and revised and edited in 2003 and 2008 in Monkstown, Ireland and New Jersey.

I want to thank my father Norman Thompson (1936-2004), and my mother Gertrude Irving-Thompson, both patrons of the arts, and my grandmother Helen Doyle-Irving (1905-1994), my brother Cliff Thompson, and my son Dylan Gerard-Wystan Thompson. I am grateful to my first teachers and mentors at the Barnstable Academy where this journey began: Paul Stittleman, Joshua Gotlieb, David Salembier and Allan Blau.

My acknowledgment to friends in Ireland, Joe Kennedy and others, who helped keep me going long enough to compose this book. A special thanks to Brendan McCormack, who was the first to see these poems during the prolific years of our correspondence. My gratitude goes out to fellow poet Kamal Ayyildiz, a friend and colleague for almost twenty-five years. His support and encouragement during many dark nights of the soul have proved immeasurable. I wish to recognize the composer Harold Budd and the influence of his music, especially that of *The White Arcades*, on the composition of this book. I want to thank Dr. Michael Milano, Tattfoo and Ensze Tan, Robert Kelly for his editorial suggestions and fortitude, Chuck Stein for his insightful reading of the manuscript and, of course, George and Susan Quasha without whom Barrytown/Station Hill Press would not exist. I am deeply indebted to Jenny Fox, the Managing Editor of Barrytown/Station Hill Press, for her faith and perseverance in this project. Her encouragement and guidance made this publication possible.

Finally, I would like to express my love and gratitude to Jennifer Lynne Poole for her support and encouragement during the many years of this journey.

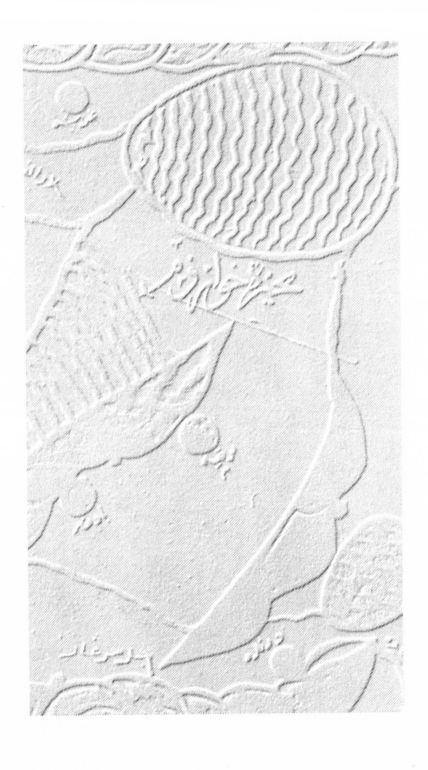

Breinigsville, PA USA
15 September 2009
224106BV00001B/9/P